THE TROJAN HORSE

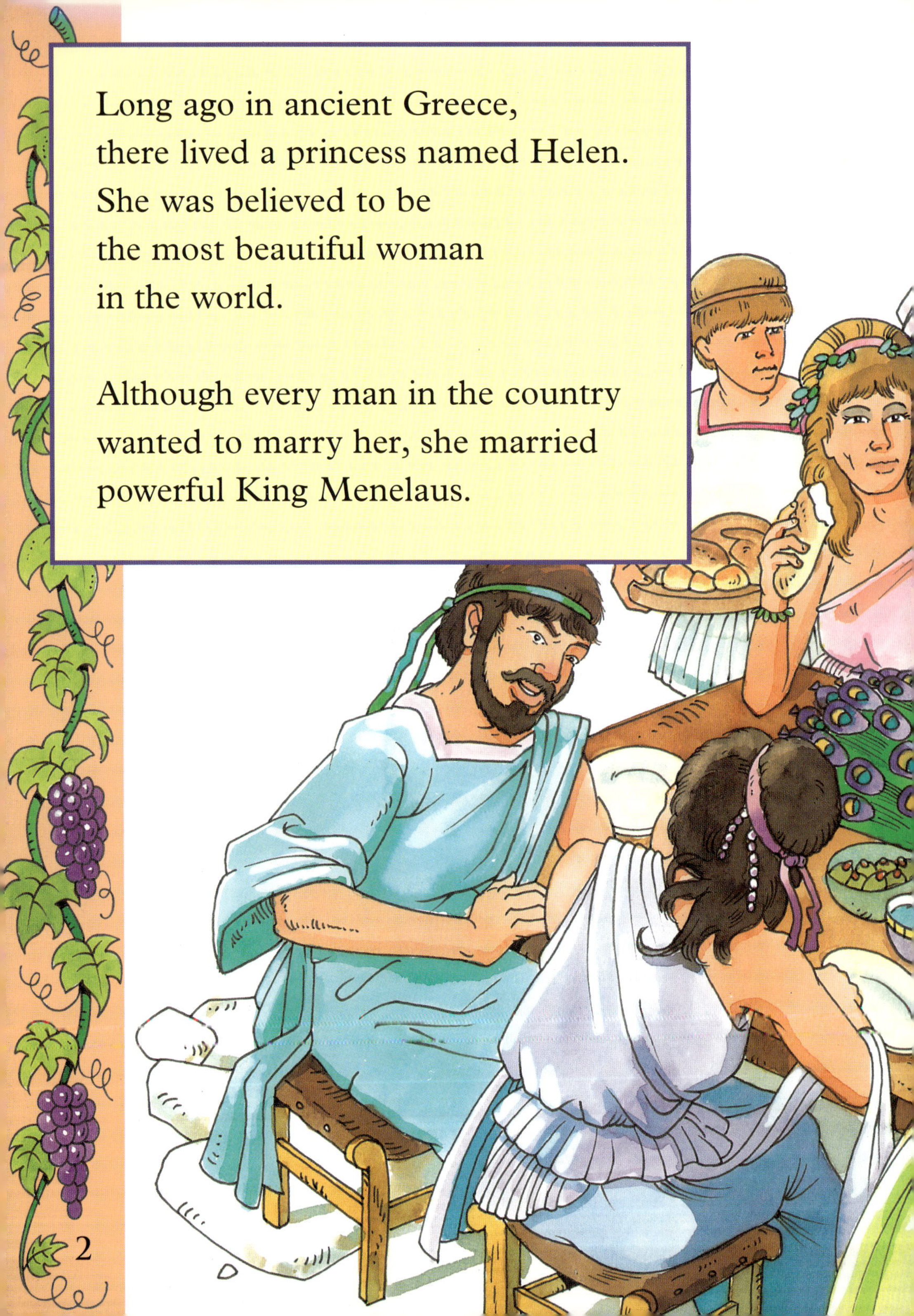

Long ago in ancient Greece,
there lived a princess named Helen.
She was believed to be
the most beautiful woman
in the world.

Although every man in the country
wanted to marry her, she married
powerful King Menelaus.

Helen and Menelaus lived happily together
until a handsome prince named Paris
came to visit their palace.
He had traveled to Greece from
the faraway city of Troy.

Paris told Helen about Troy,
and soon talked her into fleeing with him
across the sea to his homeland.

When Menelaus discovered Helen and Paris were gone, he was very angry. He went to his brother, King Agamemnon, for help.

Together, the brothers got all the other Greek chieftains to join them and declare war on Troy.

They set sail for Troy with one thousand ships.

When the Greeks landed at Troy,
they couldn't break through the walls of the city.

After many years of fighting,
the Greeks decided they needed a better plan.
They'd have to outsmart the Trojans
if they were going to win the war.

Odysseus, one of the most cunning
Greek chieftains, had an idea.
Under his orders, the men started to work.
They chopped and cut, hammered and sawed.

A few days later, the thousands of soldiers climbed back on board their ships and sailed away during the night...

or at least most of them did.

Early the next morning,
the Trojans looked for the Greeks.
They were very surprised to see
that the Greeks had gone.

They were even more surprised
to see that the Greeks had left them
a fine gift – a giant wooden horse.

The Trojans were happy. The war was over! They pulled the huge horse into their city, and feasted and danced well into the night. Finally the parties across the city ended. The Trojans collapsed, exhausted.

But not everyone in Troy was asleep.
Deep inside the wooden horse,
something stirred.

Then a trap door opened,
and a rope dropped down.
A group of fierce Greek warriors
climbed down and looked around
the sleeping city.

Stealthily, the Greeks opened the gates and let in the rest of their army, which had only pretended to sail away.

Before morning, the Greeks had taken over the entire city.

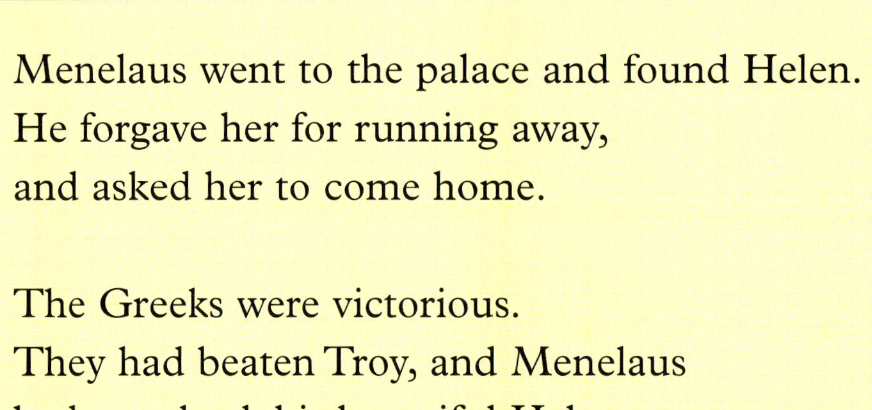

Menelaus went to the palace and found Helen.
He forgave her for running away,
and asked her to come home.

The Greeks were victorious.
They had beaten Troy, and Menelaus
had won back his beautiful Helen.

And to this day, people tell the story of the Trojan Horse, and how it helped the Greeks win the war.

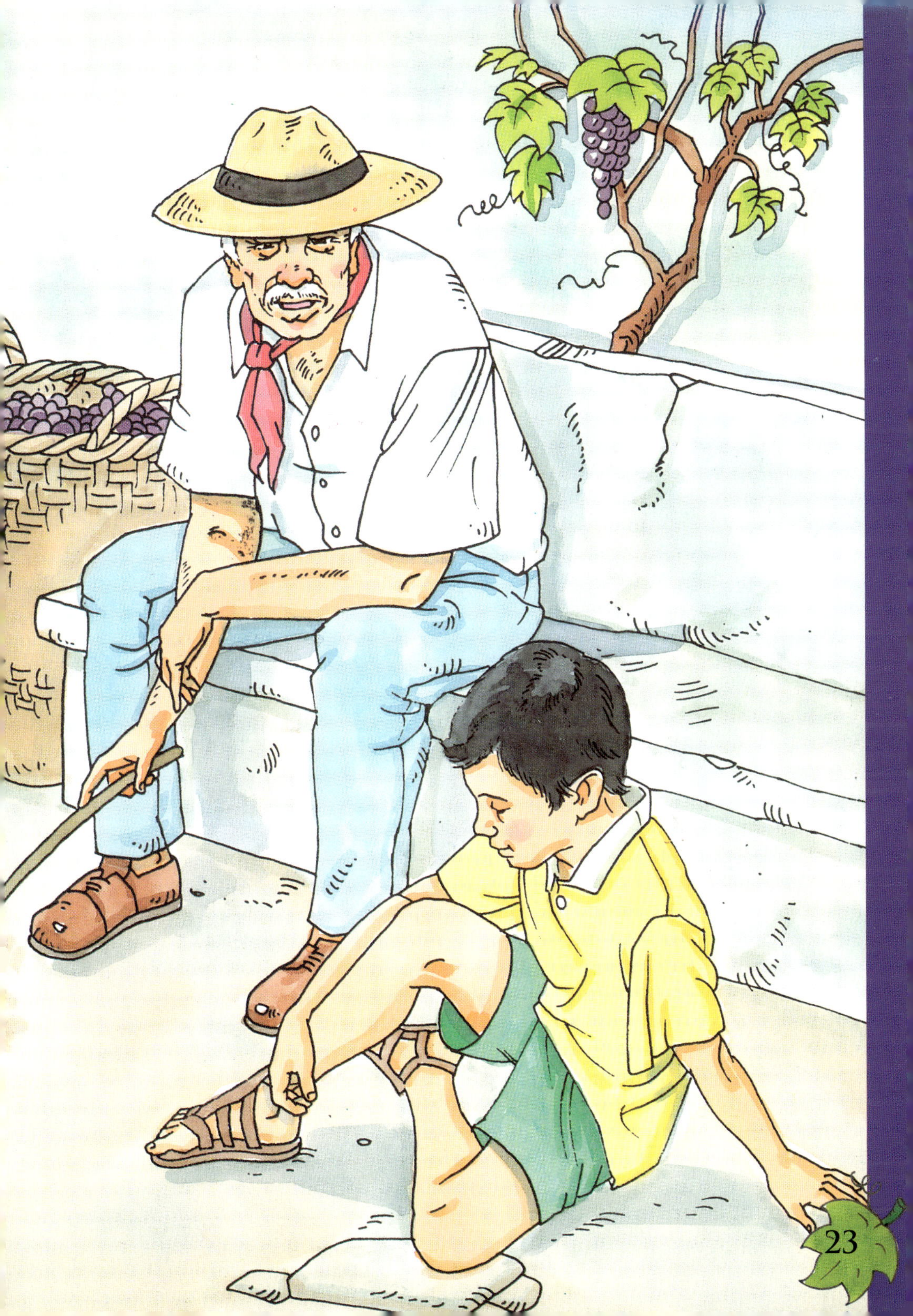

In Greek mythology, Helen of Troy was the most beautiful woman in the world, and the daughter of Zeus, the king of the gods.

According to one myth, Zeus gave Leda, a beautiful woman, a swan's egg, from which Helen was born.